SOUTHAMPTON TRAMWAYS

Martin Petch

Series editor Robert J Harley

MP Middleton Press

Cover picture: Until 1938 Southampton's medieval Bargate arch obstructed all High Street traffic, hence the unusual design of much of the tram fleet. Number 11 is the sole survivor of this dome-roof type and is being restored locally. (L.N.Smith Coll.)

Cover colours: These represent Southampton's pre-war tram livery.

To my fianceé, Veronica Yates

First published July 1994

ISBN 1 873793 33 2

© Middleton Press 1994

Design - Deborah Goodridge

Published by Middleton Press
                Easebourne Lane
                Midhurst
                West Sussex
                GU29 9AZ
                Tel: (0730) 813169
(From 16 April 1995 - (01730) 813169)

Printed & bound by Biddles Ltd,
                Guildford and Kings Lynn

CONTENTS

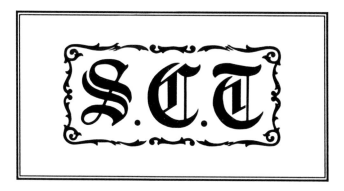

INTRODUCTION AND ACKNOWLEDGEMENTS

I am delighted to be able to produce this, the first book devoted to Southampton's tramways, especially as I was born eight years after their demise! Regular holidays in Belgium account for a lifelong passion for trams, which inevitably extended to those of my home town.

In preparing this book, my first recourse was to my own extensive postcard and photograph collection, and to those of my friends in *Tram 57 Project*, especially Nigel and Angela Smith, Glenn Day, John Horne and Bill White. Other sources include Southampton University Library, Fred Ward, David Packer, and the collection of the late Alan Watkins, with the kind permission of his widow Ann. Some material has been gleaned from the booklet "100 Years of Southampton Transport". I must also thank John Bell for his help with my queries, and Alan Stokes for letting me loose on his word processor. Godfrey Croughton

has kindly supplied many of the tickets.

The track map was produced by Angela Smith; the Ordnance Survey 25-inch map extracts are from the 1932 to 1942 editions, except Bridge Street/Bernard Street which is 1910.

In selecting the photographs I have attempted to illustrate as many locations as possible, and throughout the life of the system. I have also striven to give correct acknowledgements.

I hope that my work is a fitting tribute to all those Company and Corporation employees who proudly maintained a smart fleet of trams. Some fought for their retention but were sadly ahead of their time - Norman Stockwell, Roy Martin, Clement Robinson, to name a few.

Some of the proceeds from this book will go towards the restoration of trams 11, 38 and 57 by *Tram 57 Project* in collaboration with Southampton City Museums.

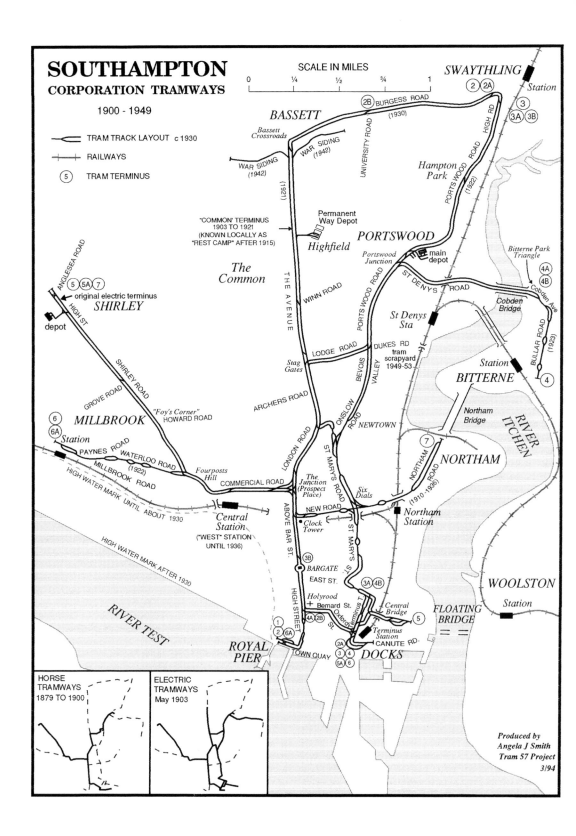

SOUTHAMPTON
CORPORATION TRAMWAYS
1900 - 1949

SCALE IN MILES

0   ¼   ½   ¾   1

— TRAM TRACK LAYOUT c 1930

+ RAILWAYS

⑤ TRAM TERMINUS

SWAYTHLING

② ②A

Station

③

③A ③B

②B BURGESS ROAD
(1930)

BASSETT

Bassett
Crossroads

WAR SIDING
(1942)

WAR SIDING
(1942)

(1921)

UNIVERSITY ROAD

Hampton
Park

PORTS WOOD ROAD

HIGH RD

(1922)

'COMMON' TERMINUS
1903 TO 1921
(KNOWN LOCALLY AS
"REST CAMP" AFTER 1915)

Permanent
Way Depot

Highfield

The
Common

THE AVENUE

WINN ROAD

PORTSWOOD

Portswood
Junction

main
depot

ST DENYS ROAD

Bitterne Park
Triangle

④A
④B

Cobden
Bridge

Cobden Ave

BULLAR ROAD
(1923)

ANGLESEA ROAD

⑤ ⑤A ⑦
← original electric terminus

SHIRLEY

HIGH ST

depot

LODGE ROAD

Stag
Gates

BEVOIS VALLEY

DUKES RD
tram
scrapyard
1949-53

St Denys
Sta

Station

④

BITTERNE

RIVER ITCHEN

SHIRLEY ROAD

GROVE ROAD

"Foy's Corner"
HOWARD ROAD

ARCHERS ROAD

ONSLOW ROAD

NEWTOWN

Northam
Bridge

⑥

⑥A

MILLBROOK

Station

PAYNES ROAD

WATERLOO ROAD
(1922)

MILLBROOK ROAD

Fourposts
Hill

COMMERCIAL ROAD

LONDON ROAD

ST MARY'S ROAD

⑦

NORTHAM ROAD

NORTHAM

(1910-1936)

HIGH WATER MARK UNTIL ABOUT 1930

Central
Station
("WEST" STATION
UNTIL 1936)

NEW ROAD

The
Junction
(Prospect
Place)

Six
Dials

Northam
Station

HIGH WATER MARK AFTER 1930

ABOVE BAR ST.

Clock
Tower

ST MARY'S ST.

RIVER TEST

③B

BARGATE
EAST ST.

Holyrood
Bemard St.

Oxford St.

Terminus T.

Central
Bridge

FLOATING
BRIDGE

WOOLSTON

Station

ST. MARY'S ST.

③A ④B

⑤

① ⑥A

④A ②B

②A

③ ④

⑤A ⑥

HIGH STREET

TOWN QUAY

ROYAL
PIER

Terminus
Station
CANUTE RD.

DOCKS

Produced by
Angela J Smith
Tram 57 Project
3/94

HORSE
TRAMWAYS
1879 TO 1900

ELECTRIC
TRAMWAYS
May 1903

GEOGRAPHICAL SETTING

Southampton has developed at the confluence of two Hampshire rivers, the Test and Itchen, which flow into Southampton Water and the Solent. The Isle of Wight's position creates a double high tide making this an ideal deep-sea port. Southampton became a city on 11 February 1964.

HISTORICAL BACKGROUND

The Romans were the first known occupants of this area, having a military camp at Clausentum - now Bitterne Manor. The Saxon town of Hamwih was located in the St Mary's area but this was later superseded by the adjacent Norman town built within walls, much of which survive.

Legend has it that pagan King Canute tried to repel the waves here; it took the London and South-Western Railway to succeed at this when they started developing the docks in the 1840s. This transformed Southampton from a sleepy little spa into a rapidly developing town.

As suburbs grew, so did the need for better public transport than the various horse bus services, and so it was that the Southampton Tramways Company opened its first route on 5 May 1879, between the Floating Bridge, The Avenue and Portswood. The Shirley route opened on 9 June. After a shaky start operation settled down until the Corporation took over in 1898 with electrification in mind.

The first electric cars ran between Shirley and the Town Junction on 22 January 1900. Soon services extended into the old town and out to St Mary's, Portswood and the Common by 1903. Between 1910 and 1923 the rest of the system was built except for the Burgess Road link which was made in 1930. The track was standard gauge.

As older residents will affectionately remember (so long as they remained seated at the time), the medieval Bargate arch presented a major obstacle to all traffic entering the High Street. Because of this, the earliest cars had a back-to-back "knifeboard" seat on the open top deck, itself lower than normal.

Initially buying from manufacturers, the Corporation opted to build its own trams from 1908: the works at Portswood produced a total of 72 up to 1932. From 1923 these had a very modern appearance when a fully-enclosed "Bargate"-type with deep-domed roof was designed. The system reached its zenith in 1930 with efficient operation, surpluses paid into the Rate Relief Fund, and smart shining trams in which the staff clearly took great pride. The fleet consisted solely of single-truck cars.

Trolleybus powers were obtained in 1937 but not exercised. During World War II the system suffered in many respects, but survived in a very dilapidated condition to limp on through the austerity years. Remaining routes were taken over by Guy "Arab" buses between May 1948 and 31 December 1949.

ROUTES

Routes as numbered in 1931:-

1   Royal Pier - Bassett - Swaythling - Docks, via High St. or via St.Marys - Swaythling - Bassett - Royal Pier.

Also: Bitterne Park - Docks via High St. - Bitterne Park via St.Marys or Bitterne Park - Docks via St.Marys - Bitterne Park via High St. (probably until 1933).

2   Royal Pier/Holy Rood - Bassett - Swaythling (1931-33, Summer only).

2A   Docks via High St. - Bassett - Swaythling (Peak-hours).

2B   Holy Rood/Bargate - Bassett - University Road (Peak-hours).

3   Swaythling - Portswood - Docks via High St. or St.Marys, returning the opposite way (1931-33 only).

3A   East St./St.Marys - Bevois Valley - Portswood - Swaythling (Sat. p.m.).

3B   Bargate - Lodge Road - Swaythling (Sat. p.m.).

4   Bitterne Park - Portswood - Docks via High St. or St.Marys, returning to Bitterne Park by the "opposite" route.

4A   Holy Rood/Bargate - Lodge Road - Portswood - Bitterne Park Triangle (Sat. p.m.).

4B   East St./St.Marys - Bevois Valley - Portswood - Bitterne Park Triangle (Sat. p.m.).

5   Floating Bridge - High St. - Shirley.

5A   Royal Pier/Docks - High St. - Shirley (Peak-hours).

6   Holy Rood - Junction - Millbrook (Later Docks via High St.).

6A   Royal Pier - Junction - Millbrook (Used after 6 became Docks).

7   Northam - Junction - Shirley.

Note: 3B and 4B did not appear on the route number blind as such.

Various workmen's services also ran; a board was hung on the dash and special fares applied.

1. Junction to Royal Pier

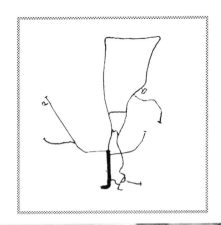

1. Our tour of the Southampton tram system starts at the Junction - here seen about 1890 as a horse tram heads north towards Portswood. Tyrrell and Green moved across Above Bar Street and still occupy the site behind the tree. (M.Petch Coll.)

2. The opening ceremony was recorded on 22 January 1900, when the electric service commenced between the Junction (Prospect Place) and Shirley. Posing proudly at the controls is Alderman Dunsford, in top hat. He was Chairman of the Tramways Committee; other Councillors are seated inside and out. (Mrs. Lee)

3. This is the scene at the Junction on Saturday 25 April 1908 after an unexpected snowstorm brought chaos and devastation to Hampshire. Trams had to be abandoned as two feet of snow fell and drifted. (M.Petch Coll.)

4. The crews of cars 67 and 91 exchange conversation as they pass Plummer Roddis, circa 1938. This store was rebuilt shortly after, only to be blitzed in 1940. Twice rebuilt, it ceased trading in July 1993. Note the third track on the little-used north junction, for specials and short workings.
(CharlesF.Klapper/Omnibus Soc.)

5. The north-bound track in the upper part of Above Bar Street is receiving attention in this early view. Car 26, of the second batch by G.F.Milnes, stops at the place indicated by the white and red markings on the ornate centre-pole. The Clock Tower was an elaborate horse-trough paid for by an animal lover in 1889. It was moved to Bitterne Park Triangle in 1935. (M.Petch Coll.)

6. A Corporation Leyland Cub, and tram 91 heading for Shirley, are seen in Above Bar about 1938. The buses carried a livery of dark blue and primrose until 1945. The Clock Tower has gone but is recalled by the tobacconist's on the left.
(C.F.Klapper/OmnibusSoc.)

7. A 1937-style tram-jam, caused by a disobedient motorist whose Morris Oxford came a poor second to the rather stouter tram 20! On the right, Marks & Spencer prepares for trade. Tram crews wait helplessly as two telegraph boys cycle past.
(Southampton University Library)

8. On a less congested occasion, tram 47 passes a beer lorry; note the splendid Art Nouveau facade next to the Cadena cafe, occupied by Permain's, House Furnishers. The centre poles were replaced with span wires about 1920. (L.N.Smith Coll.)

9. Although the town ditch and portcullis had long gone, the Bargate's low arches remained to hinder traffic; various schemes to widen the arch or demolish the whole thing were fiercely opposed by early conservationists. Car 17 heads south in the days before cycle thieves. (M.Petch Coll.)

10. The animated scene in August 1930 - how fashions have changed! (A.D.Packer Coll.)

11. This 1920s northward view from the roof of Bargate clearly illustrates the knifeboard seat on cars 44 and 61. (R.O'Donnell)

12. This view of Above Bar, again taken from the Bargate's roof, depicts the terrible destruction wrought on the town's commercial heart. (Southern Newspapers Plc.)

13. Moving south into High Street, we encounter horse car 28; sunblinds and parasols are evident, as the tram horses defiantly race a cart. In a few yards the tram will lurch leftwards onto a passing loop. (M.Petch Coll.)

14. If King George III liked trams as much as his Roman tunic, he was well-served here. From his niche he can be seen admiring the scrollwork on a centre pole. The very low Norman arch is silhouetted. (M.Petch Coll.)

15. Easy now! The date is 11 September 1923 as onlookers watch prototype dome roof car 12 squeeze through. With low headroom and a small-wheel truck, an overall height of 14ft 7ins was achieved. The track under the arch was also lowered. Percy Baker, who then became General Manager, proceeded to transform the fleet with new or rebuilt cars like this one. (M.Petch Coll.)

16. The Council at last decided in 1930 to bypass the Bargate on both flanks, and demolition of the east-side properties soon commenced. Smart flush-sided 35 comes through in about 1933. The cupola of All Saints' church is visible on the left; built in 1792 it was a casualty of 1940. (J.C.Bell Coll.)

17. Finally, in June 1938, the monument was fully bypassed and a piece of Southampton folklore was no more. Preston-built 86 would not have ventured here before, in view of its height. Ironically, the left side of the street has recently been pedestrianised! (H.Andrews)

18. Continuing towards the waterfront, car 67 coasts down the High Street past Burton's as brand new 104 gets the "clear". Very soon after, most of these buildings were demolished for the new bypass. (M.Petch)

19. The High Street is straighter today, and bland offices replace all the buildings on the left. The Star Hotel, right, happily survives as does the hulk of tram 57 after 25 years as a chicken-house. (M.Petch Coll.)

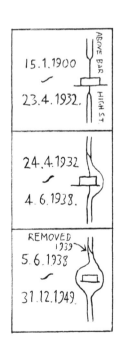

20. A little further south is the Dolphin Hotel; St.Lawrence's church, with its Victorian spire, was pulled down in 1926. (M.Petch Coll.)

21. A horse tram, one of those built by North Metropolitan Tramways, turns into Bridge Street circa 1897. Only the areas of road around the tracks and the cabs' parking are paved. (Southampton University Library)

22. Upon electrification, the tracks here were doubled, and a full triangular junction installed. The wood-block paving is well remembered by cyclists! (M.Petch Coll.)

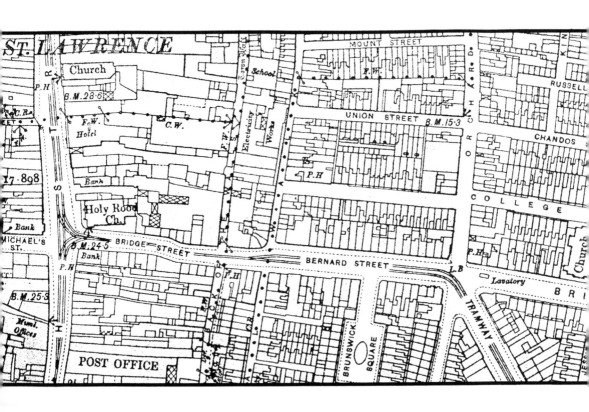

23. Beyond Holy Rood, the High Street became very narrow and the tramlines went single, then interlaced. The massive medieval vaults are all that survived the devastation of 1940. (H.B.Priestley, National Tramway Museum)

24. Unlucky 31, soon to be the tram fleet's only war casualty, here swings from Town Quay into the High Street. Note the mid-thirties livery - all red below the waistrail. (D.A.Thompson)

25. Royal Pier terminus was endowed with three tracks and a scissors crossover, which car 60 is ready to traverse. Behind are the new Western Docks then being built on reclaimed land. (C.Stevens Coll.)

THE DOCKS, SOUTHAMPTON.

27. The Town Quay was a hive of activity until the 1960s when these railway sidings were ripped up. Note the floating dock and floating crane, both centre background. (L.N.Smith Coll.)

26. The conductor has just secured number 19's trolley rope in the metal pigtail below the destination box. Behind the Harbour Board office can be seen the three funnels of RMS Queen Mary in the Eastern Docks. (A.D.Packer)

2. Docks to Bitterne Park.

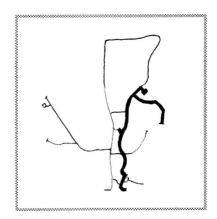

28. The Docks terminus was only a short walk from Royal Pier; tram 26 is at the end of the lines which swept round the elegant South-Western Hotel. (L.N.Smith Coll.)

30. When Bassett and Swaythling were directly linked in 1930, a circular route was introduced. Looking up Oxford Street in 1934, car 96 bears down on a cyclist prior to turning left. This street retains its elegant appearance though cyclists need no longer look out for the tram-lines. (R.Wilson)

29. Terminus Terrace is pictured in 1946, with car 68 about to depart. All the operating fleet received a coat of battleship grey in 1942 -by the late 1940s this contributed to the run-down appearance of the trams. Note the rocking bar on the overhead point frog, to set it for the curve. (D.A.Thompson)

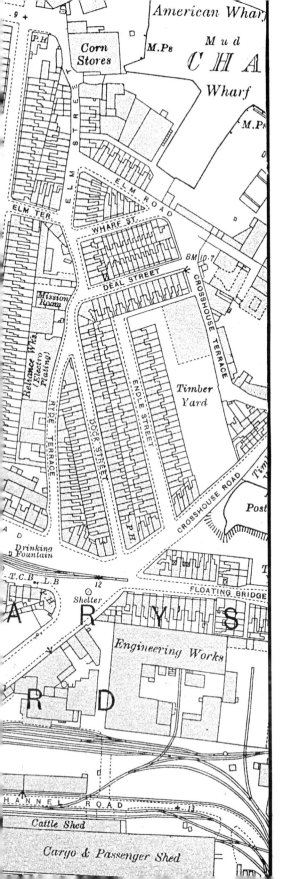

31. Looking north, 103 sets off past Terminus Station, whilst a car on route 5 is about to turn into Oxford Street, on its way from Floating Bridge to Shirley. 103 is one of the trams which received a post-war repaint in darker "bus" red and cream. (H.V.Jinks)

32. On the same junction, car 50 blocks the street helplessly - its trolley head detached from the pole. This is an enthusiasts' special, judging by the destination. (G.F.Ashwell)

34. Embroiled in the crowd, trams are held up on the curve linking Marsh Lane and St.Mary Street on 18 February 1925, at the opening of the Methodist Central Hall. (M.Petch Coll.)

33. Starting in 1940, the Light Railway Transport League hired trams on several occasions. Freshly repainted 50 is at the end of Marsh Lane on 19 May 1946; the Deanery School is behind. This north link to Floating Bridge was only used by workmen's cars from Bitterne Park or Swaythling. (A.B.Cross)

35. In 1918 six London B-class trams were bought and pressed into service. This class is fully described in the companion volume, *Greenwich and Dartford Tramways*. Number 77 is seen outside St. Mary's church still in LCC livery shortly after. (G.Day Coll.)

36. St.Mary Street is still a lively shopping area whose appearance has not altered significantly. Kingsland market is to the left of the passing loop. There is evidence of an earlier derailment in the foregrond. (A.J.Watkins Coll.)

37. There had been a crossing at Six Dials but this was removed when the Northam route succumbed. Freshly painted 99 dissects the roundabout which was later created. (A.D.Packer)

38. A connection existed in Bellevue Terrace to link St.Mary's Road with the Avenue. Used only by school, football and other specials, the tracks soon filled with dirt. As a result 81 is in trouble, so the conductor is completing the circuit with the point-iron! This was another enthusiasts' tour, on 1 June 1947. (A.D.Packer)

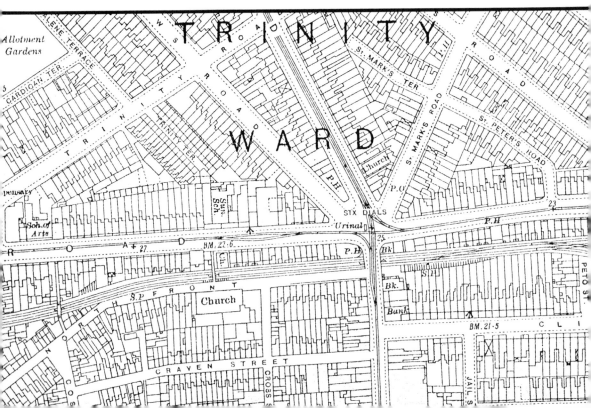

39. Bevois Valley takes the name of Southampton's legendary giant Sir Bevis, who was supposedly buried in this locality. (G.Day Coll.)

40. At the start of Portswood Road we see the remains of the Bevois Valley/Lodge Road junction. On Saturday 4 February 1950, number 21 is being transferred from Shirley depot to Portswood. This was the very last movement on the tramways. (J.C.Bell)

41. Still referred to as Portswood Junction, this area is a major suburban shopping centre. Most of these buildings survive except for the Palladium cinema of 1913, recalled in this mid-thirties postcard. (M.Petch Coll.)

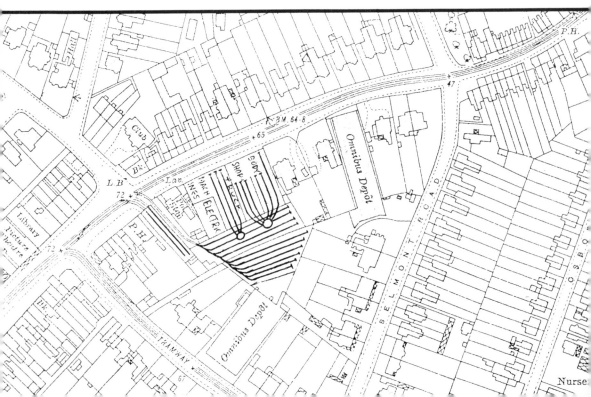

42. In 1900, Portswood Depot was converted from horse traction. Notice 14's destination plate, the trellis gate on the platform and the early lifeguard equipment. Many of these cars received full canopies around 1910. (M.Petch Coll.)

43. Fitters and crew pause inside the depot circa 1915. Milnes car 8, already 15 years old, has developed a pronounced sag; it managed to survive until 1924. The workshops were accessed via two turntables.
(Mrs.M.Corbishley/Solent Transport Trust)

44. Like many undertakings, Southampton Corporation recruited lady conductors during World War I. In May 1915 the first five pose for posterity. Note the older crest design and side destination boards then in use; it seems as if the signwriter hasn't yet finished the advert.
(Mrs.M.Corbishley/S.T.T.)

45. Car 19 certainly won't get far from the truck
shop, separated from its Peckham P35 truck.
(A.D.Packer)

46. Proceeding along St.Denys Road on a wintry post-war day, number 11 has virtually reached the end of the long climb away from Cobden Bridge, by Belmont Road. (W.C.F.White Coll.)

47. St.Denys Road is still quite narrow where it passes the Public Elementary School near the parish church; double track occupied the whole of the road. (Southampton University Library)

48. The original terminus of this route - opened 30 August 1902 - was here at Bitterne Park Triangle. On 26 July 1923 an extension to Bitterne Station was inaugurated - about ten years later 108 is climbing into Cobden Avenue, past the recently transplanted Clock Tower. (M.Petch Coll.)

49. Outsize car 81 was unique: with five bays and short, open platforms it may have been designed as a bogie car. Here it is on the passing loop at the top of Bullar Road in 1946. (A.D.Packer)

50. Bitterne Park terminus on a rainy Easter Sunday, 5 April 1942. Car 21 is on a LRTL special. Both 21 and 3 had recently had their upper decks painted grey - also note the dash-mounted side lights, masked headlight and white paint on fenders and traction poles. This route closed on 15 May 1948. (N.Stockwell Coll.)

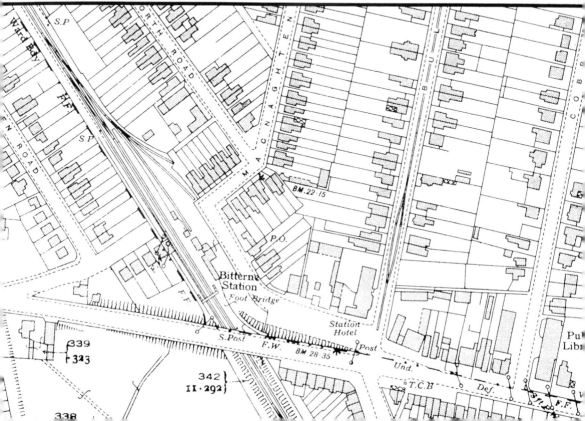

3. Junction to Bassett and Portswood

Having covered much of the eastern side of the network, we now move back to the Junction and head north.

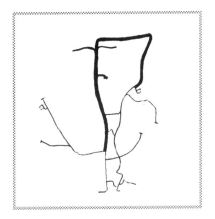

51. Chandler's was a well-known local photographer who captured pre-war Southampton in a series of beautifully detailed plates. The Victorian Central Library at the start of London Road received a direct hit in 1940. Knifeboard car 61 passes it in 1930. (D.Green Coll.)

52. The west side of London Road has changed drastically since this Edwardian summer scene was captured on film. Milnes car 2 is passing St.Paul's, an early "Gothick Revival" structure. (W.C.F.White Coll.)

SOUTHAMPTON CORPORATION TRAMWAYS

Sq   0792

1d

SOUTHAMPTON CORPORATION TRAMWAYS.
1d TICKET. Valid to Station opposite punch-hole on day of issue only. Issued subject to the Corporation Bye-laws and Regulations. Not Transferable.

West Station	Stag Gates
Shirley	Roberts Rd
Grove Road	
Winn Road	Prospect
Spring Cres.	Place
Howard Rd	Ozle
Mansion Rd	Road
Roberts Rd	East Street
Stag Gates	Northam Stn
West Station	Holy
O.S.O.	Rood
Prospect	Northam
Place	Docks or Pier
East Street	
Pier	Floating Bdg
Holy	Six Dials via
Rood	Docks Stn
Millbrook	West Station
	Grove Road
Roberts Rd	O.S.O.
Bassett	Stag Gates
Highfield Rd	
Portswood J	O.S.O.
Swaythling	
Bittern Prk	Portswood
Triangle	Junction
St. Agnes Ch	
Highfield Rd	Spring
Adelaide Rd	Crescent
Bowden Lne	Cedar Road
Portswood	Ecel Rd B Vly
Junction	Bellevue Rd
Northam	(B Vly)
Station	Holy Rood
Spring	via Clock Tr
Crescent	Northam Stn
Earls Rd B V	via B. Vly
Bellevue Rd	East St St M
St. M	Deks. Float
Triangle	ing Bg Nthm
Adelaide Rd	Bowden Lne
Northam	St. Agnes Ch
Clock	Deks via St M
Tower	Est Stor Byne
	Rd St M via St D

53. The band of the Hants Royal Garrison Artillery hired a tram to recruit in 1915. The Ordnance Survey headquarters behind was to be yet another victim of the next conflict. (W.C.F.White,"Southampton Pictorial Record")

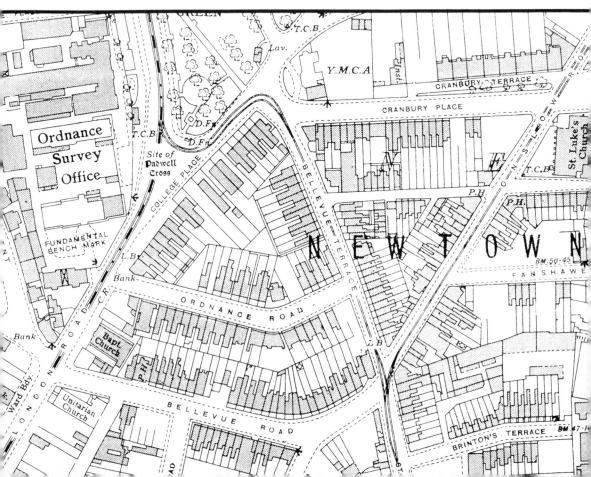

54. Football specials lying in wait at College Place, probably in 1947. A sight to stir enthusiasts.... the line-up includes two ex-LCC cars. (A.J.Watkins Coll.)

55. The football specials would move up The Avenue to Archers Road at the appointed time, to pick up the happy crowds - Saints beat Barnsley 3-0 on 26 February 1949. (A.F.Cook/A.J.WatkinsColl.)

56. In a more sedate era, the elegant centre-poles are being repainted by two men. Tram 47 keeps on appearing in these old postcards! (M.Petch Coll.)

57. Dome car 20 has turned out of Lodge Road to join The Avenue at "Stag Gates". (L.N.Smith Coll.)

58. Even today this area is called Stag Gates. Here they are, before their removal in June 1919. They marked the entrance to Bevois Park, one of several large estates which were parcelled off for housing development a century ago. (Photomatic Ltd.)

59. The Avenue - more prosaically the A33 - must rank as one of the finest approach roads into any town. It was built through the Common in the 18th century and tree-lined. The foliage forms a canopy over tram 38, picking up at the Westwood Road stop in the early twenties. The body of this tram survived and will be restored to uncanopied condition. (M.Petch Coll.)

60. Another fine postcard of The Avenue
bathed in summer sun in the 1930s. Until 1921
this was the terminus, known as "Rest Camp"
since an army camp existed on the Common
during the 1914-18 war. Speeds of up to 35 mph
could be reached along here. (M.Petch Coll.)

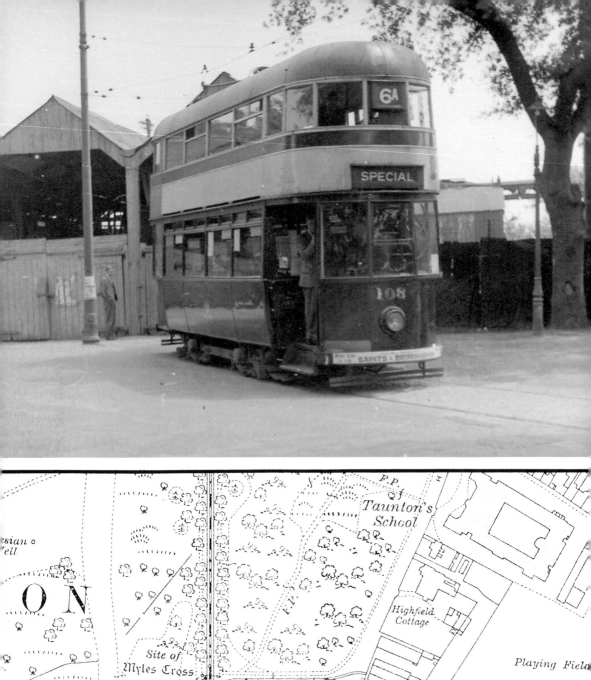

61. No enthusiasts' trip was complete without a visit to the tram shed in Highfield Road. But where's the key? (A.J.Watkins Coll.)

62. This small depot was used for permanent way duties, one of its residents being this works car, formerly "knifeboard" 22. Painted dark brown, it served as a welding and engineering vehicle, surviving to the bitter end. (A.F.Cook/A.J.Watkins Coll.)

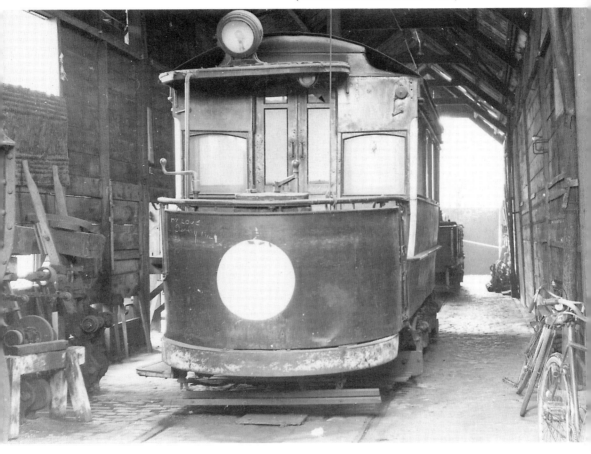

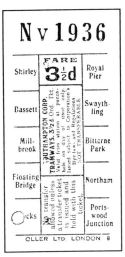

63. Following the worst of the Blitz, operators were urged to store some vehicles away from built-up areas. Accordingly, two long sidings were laid in Bassett woods, at the northern extremity of the Common, in 1942. This is the east siding on 20 September of that year, with newly-painted cars 68 and 76 in the foreground. As well as enthusiasts, courting GIs found the parked trams of great interest! (J.E.Gready)

64. "Preston" 85 gets ready to give its best speed from the top of The Avenue. The disused wartime siding is to the right. (F.E.J.Ward)

65. Burgess Street was a country lane until 1930 when the last tramway extension was laid - seen here at University Road. New garden fences are in place; pavements and overhead wires will follow. (N.Gardiner)

66. Brand-new 109 with its early route number
stencil glides along Burgess Road in 1931.
What a superb sight! (R.Elliott)

67. Car 96 heads east on new route 1 on Thursday 10 July 1930. Familiar ball-and-spike finials have yet to be rammed into these two poles. The University has recently extended onto the area behind the tram. (N.Gardiner)

68. A large new council estate was built to the north of Burgess Road - and provided with cheap, reliable public transport (until1949). In this late 1930s view, car 93 is at the foot of the hill and about to turn sharp right into High Road, Swaythling; this is before the era of unsightly UPVC windows! (B.Elliot)

69. Between 1922 and 1930, Swaythling terminus was at the far end of High Road. Car 103 will head left at that point. (F.E.J.Ward)

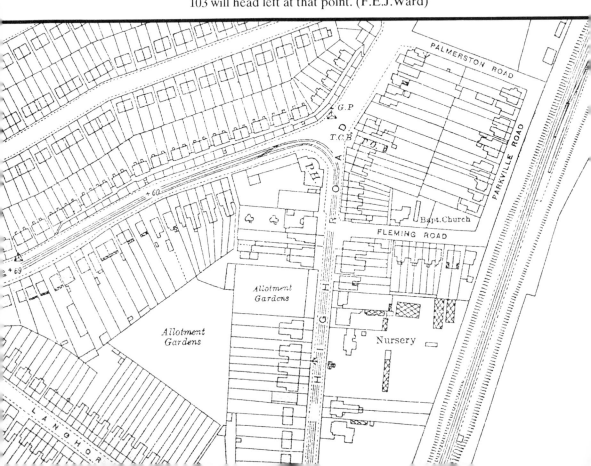

70. Not so many pictures seem to exist showing some stretches of routes, but 102 here descends Portswood Road, southbound, near Harrison Road. Cyclists had to endure granite setts until the tramlines were removed. (A.D.Packer/J.C.Bell Coll.)

71. Milnes "garden seat" 33 seen further down, outside the original iron church of the Immaculate Conception; Hampton Park terminus was a little to the north. In their original form these trams could not pass under the Bargate, operating instead on the eastern routes. (B.J.Ticehurst Coll.)

4. Northam and Millbrook Routes

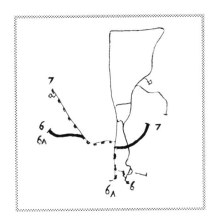

73. During and after World War I the Northam route became busier and was worked as Shirley - Northam, later numbered 7. This was the preserve of the "flat toppers", being a route which avoided the Bargate. Motorman Percy Wrixon proudly stands at the controls of 91 at Northam in August 1933. The terminus was just short of the old wooden bridge over the Itchen. (M.J.O'Connor)

72. The tramway linking Clock Tower to Northam opened on 17 December 1910 and was at first operated as a shuttle, using two demi-cars 50 and 51; these were rebuilt from horse trams. The crew of 51 pose in New Road not long after inauguration. (G.Day Coll.)

74. Illuminated cars were a feature of many tramways, and Southampton proudly partook of this tradition. Apart from the annual carnival, other events were duly celebrated. This is probably car 14, at Northam on the occasion of King George V's silver jubilee in May 1935. The Northam route closed on 4 June 1936. (Miss F.Harris/J.C.Bell Coll.)

75. A branch to Millbrook was opened on 5 January 1922, becoming route 6/6A. This only lasted until October 1935, apart from workmen's services which continued up to 1947. Car 72's impeccable lining can be admired as it stands outside Millbrook Station in 1930. (R.Elliott)

76. On 13 June 1948 car 108, on a Southern Counties Touring Society special, must have made one of the last trips over the line to Millbrook. This scene has now been drastically altered by road "improvements". (Southampton City Museums)

77. Reportedly on the Millbrook route, Driving Instructor Wheeler initiates a group of ladies into the motorman's skills in the early years of World War II. Ellen Sawyer is to his right. Should any reader have a photograph of a tram in Waterloo Road..... (M.Petch Coll.)

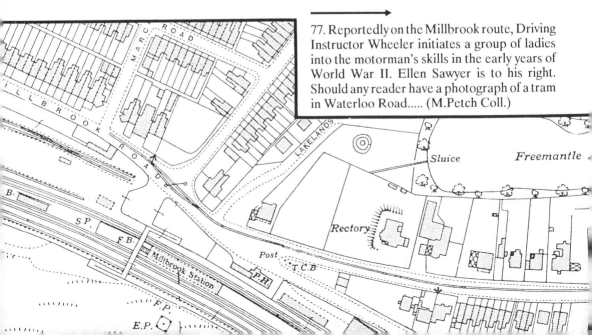

5. Floating Bridge to Shirley

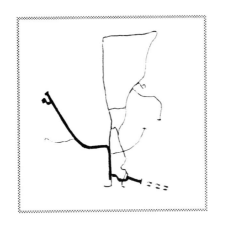

78. The floating bridge was a chain ferry which linked Southampton to Woolston between 1836 and 1977, when the Itchen Bridge was opened. Operated by the Corporation from 1934, it was the nearest thing to a floating tram. (J.B.Horne Coll.)

79. As the floating bridge passengers walked up to the terminus, the next tram would suddenly make off! The elaborate fountain disappeared along with the trams, and this site is now buried under the road linking Central Bridge to the Itchen Bridge. (J.H.Meredith/A.J.Watkins Coll.)

←

80. Central Bridge, spanning the railway, was built in 1882. It carried electric trams from 1901, whereupon the horse tramway in Canute Road was abandoned. 104 grinds round the curve from Terminus Terrace; the destination "Shirley" has already been set.
(Southampton City Museums)

←

81. Shirley-bound trams then turned right into Oxford Street outside Terminus Station. In this Edwardian scene a Milnes knifeboard tram passes the "Grapes" public house, today a trendy place to meet. In those days it was thronged by seamen and ladies of the night. (W.C.F.White Coll.)

82. The spires of St. Michael's and Holy Rood grace the skyline in Bernard Street; this postcard shows the busy scene in about 1913. In the side streets, people lived in cramped, dismal housing. (M.Petch Coll.)

83. The night of 30 November 1940 changed the face of Southampton for ever. Tram 31 was welded to the rails in the cauldron that was previously Bernard Street.
(Southern Newspapers Plc.)

84. The line to Royal Pier was closed for security reasons in 1941, but reopened in 1945. It saw little further use after the Bassett route closed on 5 March 1949; car 15 is reversing on the single line outside the battle-scarred Head Post Office. The destination reads "Holy Rood": that church's ruins are to the right of the tram. (H.B.Priestley)

85. On our last trip through the town centre we round the west side of the Bargate. Flower baskets were fitted to traction poles to celebrate King George VI's coronation.
(C.F.Klapper/Omnibus Soc.)

86. Car 74 speeds up Above Bar past some fine twentieth century architecture; of all these buildings only two remain today. Successions of planners and developers have finished off what the Luftwaffe missed.
(Southampton University Library)

87. Turning left at the Junction, trams stop outside the Civic Centre Art Gallery. On 18 June 1948, dome-roof car 18 has broken down and will be pushed by poor old 65 all the way to Shirley! Meanwhile the author's mother (in a white coat, left) is about to board 65.
(A.B.Cross)

88. The track is receiving attention as car 2 heads east along Commercial Road. A Southampton feature was the use of the fender for adverts, usually football fixtures or cycle races, but it's Beginners' night at the Ice Rink to-night! (J.Pullen)

89. The "dip" in Commercial Road was much more pronounced in tramway days. On 8 January 1949 cars 18, 16 and 98 prove that "there's always a tram in sight"! (A.D.Packer)

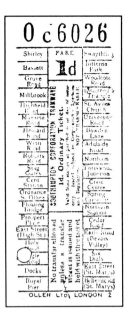

90. The SCTS special of 13 June 1948 picks up its passengers on Fourposts Hill - the nearest point to the Central Station - and will head back over the crossover. Opposite Hill Lane stood the Hill Top Inn. (Lens of Sutton)

91. Having climbed Fourposts Hill, for which horse trams required an extra trace-horse, we proceed along Shirley Road and soon reach the junction with the Millbrook route at Waterloo Road. An engineer would today describe this rail as being "life-expired". (H.B.Priestley/N.T.M.)

92. Returning to the Blitz, car 13 didn't reach Floating Bridge - its roof was blasted off in Shirley Road near to Languard Road. The tram was subsequently repaired but took poor old 31's fleet number! (H.Lourdes-Cresswell Coll.)

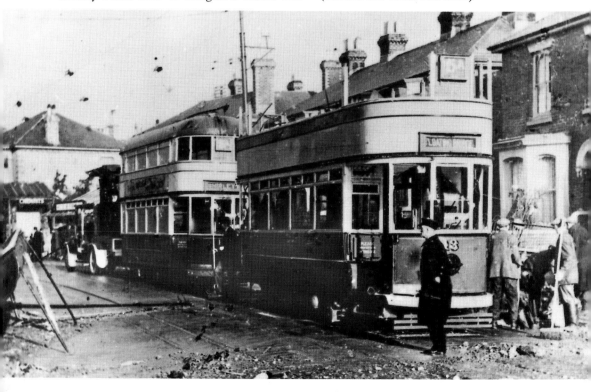

SOUTHAMPTON CORPORATION TRAMWAYS.

NOTICE !!

SHIRLEY SECTION

Reconstruction of the Permanent Way for Electric Traction.

On and after WEDNESDAY NEXT, JULY 12th, 1899 (until further notice) the Shirley Cars to and from Town and Portswood will run to

KINGSTON ROAD ONLY

Busses will run to and from Kingston Road and Shirley.

A Transfer Service cannot there be guaranteed, but every effort will be made to meet the public convenience.

GEORGE B. CARNON, Manager.

Municipal Offices, July 3rd, 1899.

BY ORDER.

"Southampton Times" Steam Printing Works, 70, Above Bar.

93. After Foy's Corner, Shirley Road is ruler-straight. Buildings soon linked the once separate village during the early tramway era. The Atherley picture house, centre, was one of three in this vicinity. The presence of soldiers at left is explained by the nearby POW camp. (L.N.Smith Coll.)

94. Shirley High Street has not altered much since 1938, although the traffic volume could again benefit from the discipline imposed by the trams, in their predestined grooves! (A.J.Watkins Coll.)

95. Four different track layouts existed at Shirley terminus; in this early view looking back along the High Street, the original centre poles have been removed. (C.Carter Coll.)

B d 1517		
Shirley	FARE	Swaythling
Bassett	1½d	Tubeice Park
Grove Road		Woodcote Road
Millbrook		Portton Terr.
Highfield Road		St Agnes Church
Mansion Road		University Road
Winn Road		Bowden Lane
Winn Road		Adelaide Road
Kings Road		Northam
Stag Gates		Portswood Junction
Cent Station		Civic Centre
Ordnance S. Office		Spring Crescent
Floating Bridge		Northam Station
Prospect Place		Cedar Road
East Street (High St.)		Earls Road (Bevois Valley)
Holy Road		Six Dials
Oxle Road		East Street (St. Marys)
Docks		Bellevue Rd (St. Marys)
Royal Pier		

SOUTHAMPTON CORPORATION TRAMWAYS. 1½d. Ordinary Ticket. Valid from station at which issued and only. No transfer allowed unless a transfer ticket is issued and held with this ticket.

OLLER LTD LONDON 2

A 9645		
Shirley	FARE	Broadlands Road
Bassett	2½d	Swaything
Grove Road		Bitterne Park
Millbrook		Woodcote Road
Highfield Road		St. Agnes Church
Mansion Road		Bitterne Pk. Triangle
Winn Road		Bowden Lane
Roberts Road		Adelaide Road
Stag Gates		Northam
Central Station		Portswood Junction
Ordnance Office		Spring Crescent
Prospect Pl Junction		Northam Station
Floating Bridge		Cedar Road
Holy Road		Earls Road (Bevois Vly)
East Street (High St.)		Six Dials
Oxle Road		East Street (St. Marys)
Docks		Bellevue Rd (St. Marys)
Royal Pier		

SOUTHAMPTON CORPORATION TRAMWAYS. 2½d. Ordinary Ticket. Valid from station at which issued and only. Issued subject to Corporation Byelaws. NOT TRANSFERABLE. No transfer allowed unless a transfer ticket is issued and held with this ticket.

OLLER LTD LONDON 3

96. The second track layout - including this curve into Park Street - can be seen as the crew of car 13 changes ends. (A.D.Packer Coll.)

97. Around 1910 the terminus was extended by one block to the end of Anglesea Road. A bland pedestrianised area now occupies the left side of the street. (L.N.Smith Coll.)

Shirley High Street, Southampton.

98. Finally, a scissors crossover was added beyond Anglesea Road. Car 21 on that 1942 special shares the stub terminus with 16 -adverse weather rarely deters tram fans! A local had spotted them taking pictures at Floating Bridge - then a restricted area - and when the group returned to Waterloo Station they were promptly arrested! (J.C.Bell Coll.)

99. The first LRTL tour in Southampton was on 19 May 1940. Did they spare a thought for the Army (including the author's father) being chased to Dunkirk? This is Carlisle Road, at the back of the Regent Cinema. (J.C.Gillham)

100. Crews come on duty in the early afternoon as car 54 is made ready for service. Most of the dome-roof cars worked from Portswood, leaving Shirley with older stock. This was because Shirley depot would only accommodate four shorter cars per track, if you wanted to pull down the shutters as well! (A.D.Packer Coll.)

101. Bill Knopp (left) and Norman Stockwell (right) were among several activists who opposed the Council's post-war anti-tram policy; Norman spent the rest of his life crusading for better public transport. Housing now occupies the site of the depot. The road is Settle Close - just what the trams did at night. (A.D.Packer)

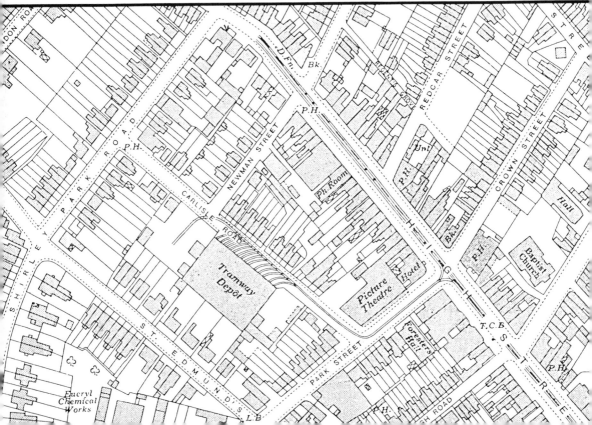

6. Finale

102. "Dog sees ghost tram in Shirley" - in fact it's in undercoat, turning into Carlisle Road prior to being transported to Leeds in July 1949. Although all cars on Peckham trucks were sold to Leeds, only eleven entered service. Some never left Southampton whilst others were diverted to a Yorkshire pig farm! The London "Felthams" were a more attractive purchase. (A.J.Watkins)

103. The oldest trams met their end in the siding by Shirley depot during the late 40s. Remaining uncanopied cars - such as 52, Portswood's first home-built effort - were never painted grey. (M.Petch Coll.)

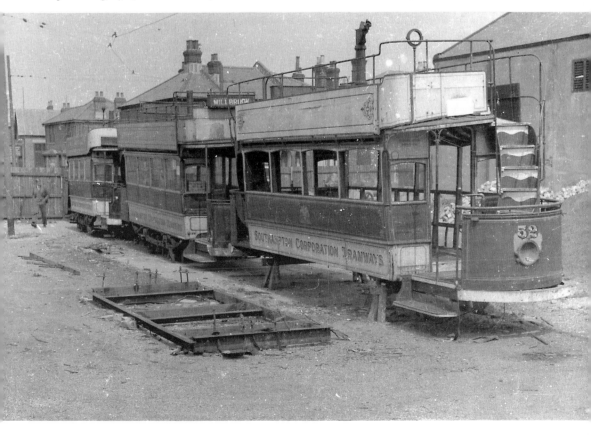

104. All good things come to an end, and the end came on 31 December 1949. During that day car number 9 toured remaining route 5 in special farewell attire. Shoppers at the Junction pause, smiling affectionately, as they witness the close of a chapter in the town's life. (F.E.J.Ward)

105. A dismal day in Briggate, Leeds. On 21 February 1950 exiled 295 (ex SCT 104) will turn right into Boar Lane, while 290 (ex 108) passes on its way to Moortown. Although these trams rode well on the Leeds reserved tracks, their low ceilings made people think Sotonians were pygmies! (R.B.Parr)

106. Apart from the sales to Leeds, nearly all of the other trams were purchased by A.F.Harris, whose scrapyard was next to Mount Pleasant railway sidings. Still enjoying its glory-days, the Bournemouth Belle accelerates past in the care of a Merchant Navy class loco. Meanwhile, tram 70 awaits its fate. (Lens of Sutton)

107. Following the success of those special trips, the LRTL decided that a knifeboard tram should be saved, and car 45 was bought in 1948 for the sum of £10. This was the start of a long story ending at Crich, our national tram museum, where number 45 has a place of honour. (M.Petch)

108. Meanwhile tram 11, withdrawn in 1947, went to the graveyard but was sold on and survived as a wendy-house until brought back to Southampton in 1979 for reconstruction. A replacement truck has been obtained from Porto and suitably modified. Knifeboard cars 38 and 57 are also awaiting restoration by *Tram 57 Project*. (M.Petch)

7. Rolling Stock

109. Pictorial records show that the horsecar fleet was quite varied, cars having between four and seven bays; the highest fleet number was 28. Number 12's glass adverts show up well as the Company's key staff pose for the camera, circa 1889. (Mrs.G.Gould)

KNIFEBOARD TYPE

110. A total of 63 of these cars were built, first by Milnes and Hurst Nelson, then at Portswood works. From 1909 full canopies were fitted and many older cars were modified to match. Number 60 dates from 1910. (Lacey's Studios)

111. Even in 1900 the knifeboard seat design was an obsolete feature of the horse tram era, dictated by the Bargate. (A.F.Cook)

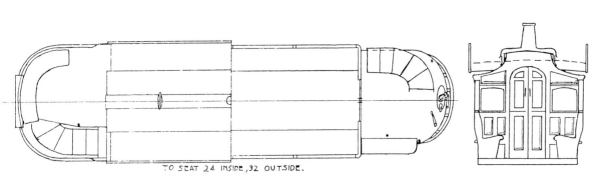

TO SEAT 24 INSIDE, 32 OUTSIDE.

Car 57

MILNES GARDEN-SEAT TYPE

112. Numbers 30 to 37 were built by G.F. Milnes and had open top decks with half-canopies. Two later received open-balcony top covers and all were completely rebuilt in 1929/30 as dome-roof cars, retaining three lower deck bays. (C.Stevens Coll.)

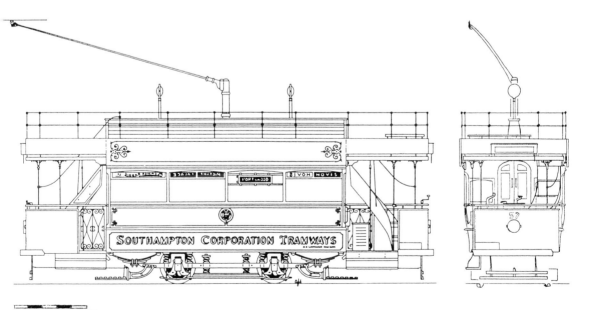

0 1 2 3 4 FEET

113. In 1918, six LCC B-class trams were acquired, complete with fully-enclosed top covers. Needed on Bargate routes in 1923, the top covers were removed and the upper deck structure lowered by seven inches. Grey-clad 80 is entering the very narrow access to Portswood depot; behind is the works facade. (M.Petch Coll.)

PRESTON CARS

114. Cars 82-91 were built by Dick Kerr & Co. of Preston in 1919 to a standard design. Restricted from the High Street until 1938, they worked other routes. Most of one end of tram 87 survives for eventual display. (R.Elliott)

115. A total of 51 dome-roof trams were built at Portswood, or rebuilt from other cars. Later versions had upholstered reversible seats and being "home-made", no two were quite the same. A complete fleet list, including the complex 1920s renumbering, is beyond the scope of this book. (M.Petch Coll.)

116. The spartan interior of car 51, with plenty of varnish, was typical of the fleet. (F.E.J.Ward)

117. Cars 104-109 were eight feet wide, allowing two-and-two seating in both decks. Although 109 was the highest fleet number, a further six cars took vacant numbers in 1931/32. All of these had air brakes, which were removed during World War II, after a runaway in Burgess Road. (M.J.O'Connor)

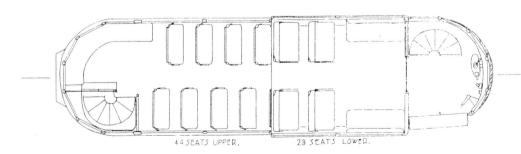

44 SEATS UPPER,   28 SEATS LOWER.

Dome Car 104

118. Two open works cars were built in 1908; one survived to the very end, and was captured on film outside Plummers in the austerity years; an impatient Guy Arab bus is following. A toastrack car was also built in 1916 but was soon sold, to Portsmouth. (A.B.Cross)

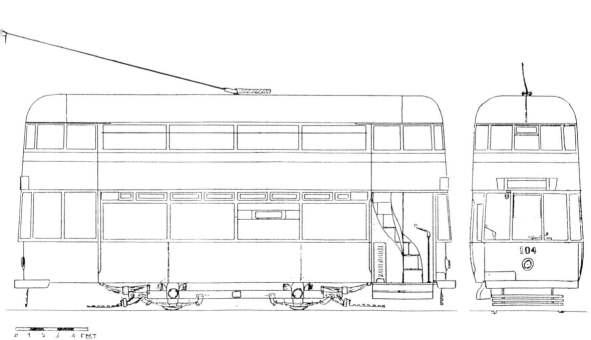

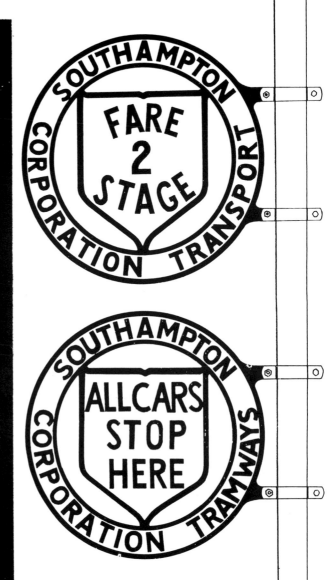

SWAYTHLING
DOCKS VIA ST MARY'S
DOCKS VIA HIGH ST
BITTERNE PARK
SHIRLEY
NORTHAM
FLOATING BRIDGE
PORTSWOOD
ROYAL PIER
HOLY ROOD
MILLBROOK
BASSETT
SPECIAL
BITTERNE TRIANGLE
EAST ST (ST MARY'S)
JUNCTION
WINN ROAD
BARGATE
HAMPTON PARK
UNIVERSITY RD

SOUTHAMPTON CORPORATION TRANSPORT — FARE 2 STAGE

SOUTHAMPTON CORPORATION TRAMWAYS — ALL CARS STOP HERE

TRAM SERVICES.				First Car. A.M.	Last Car. P.M.	Intervals. Early Morn. Mins.	Other times. Mins.
WEEKDAYS.							
Shirley—Floating Bridge	...	...	...	5. 5	10.32	10	4
Floating Bridge—Shirley	...	...	...	5.35	10.57	10	4
Swaythling—Pier *via* Bassett		...	...	7.10	10.30	6	8
Pier—Swaythling *via* Bassett		...	...	7.40	11. 0	6	8
Swaythling—Docks *via* Bassett and High St.				5.15	7. 5 A.M.		
SUNDAYS.							
Shirley—Floating Bridge	...	...	...	10. 7	10.32	15	5
Floating Bridge—Shirley	...	...	...	10.39	10.57	15	5
Swaythling—Pier *via* Bassett		...	...	10. 3	10.30	15	6 & 8
Pier—Swaythling *via* Bassett		...	...	10.35	11. 0	15	6 & 8

8. Power Supply

119. Western Esplanade generating station worked from 1903 until the 1970s. This 1930s view also shows the new facade of West Station, renamed Central in 1935. The sea orig- inally reached here and at least once flooded the generating station, stopping the trams. (Southampton Corporation/J.B.Horne)

FLOATING BRIDGE SERVICES.

Weekdays.

6.0 to 6.45 a.m., every 7½ minutes.
7.45 a.m. to 4.45 p.m., every 7½ minutes.
5.45 to 11 p.m., every 7½ minutes.
1 a.m. to 5 a.m., every 30 minutes.

6.45 to 7.45 a.m., every 6 minutes.
4.45 to 5.45 p.m., every 6 minutes.
11 p.m. to 1 a.m., every 15 minutes.
5 a.m. to 6 a.m., every 15 minutes.

Sundays.

6 to 10 a.m., every 15 minutes, remainder of day as above.
The bridges maintain a 24-hour daily service across the river Itchen.

120. The Corporation was allowed to string an overhead wire along the Southern Railway's siding which served the power station. A home-made loco was used for many years, but in 1930 BTH supplied this machine for £1139, although it was actually built by Baguley (Engineers) Ltd of Burton-on-Trent. (L.Tavender)

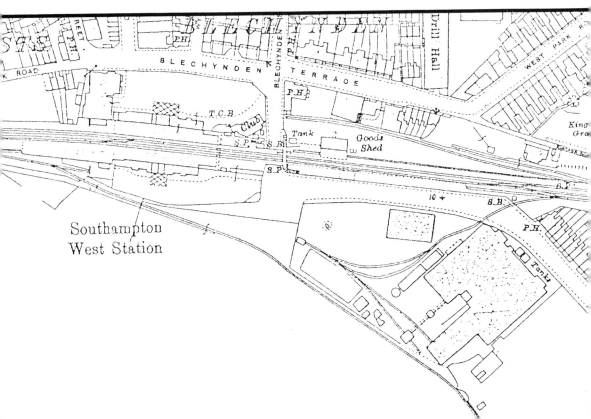

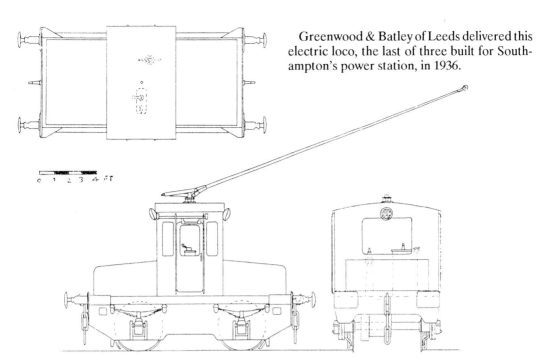

Greenwood & Batley of Leeds delivered this electric loco, the last of three built for Southampton's power station, in 1936.

9. Tailpiece

121. *"A thousand ages in thy sight*
Are like an evening gone,
Short as the watch that ends the night
Before the rising sun."

Isaac Watts, born in Southampton in 1674. An apt quotation for this final view at Floating Bridge on 31 December 1949. (F.E.J.Ward)